i P

The User Guide For all iPhone 8, iPhone 8 Plus and older

iPhone model Users

Jhale Binjeh

ISBN: 978-1-63750-239-6

Table of Contents

Introduction

This book is the best user manual you need to guide you on how to use and optimally maximize your iPhone.

Millions of people all over the world are iPhone users! Simply because iPhone cell phone is a hugely popular smartphone that offers many advances and convenient features, including a *camera like no other*, *Siri*, turn-by-turn driving directions, a calendar, and a lot more. But if you're acquiring the iPhone 8, and iPhone 8 Plus, for the first time, or you probably need more information on how to use your device optimally, and that is why this book is your best companion.

The easy-to-follow steps in this book would help you manage, personalize, and communicate better using your new iPhone 8, and iPhone 8 Plus cell phone optimally.

In this book, you would learn;

- iPhone 8 correct set-up process

- iPhone 8 Plus Features

- How to personalize your iPhone

- How to fix common iPhone 8 problems

- 23 Top iPhone Tips and Tricks

- iPhone 8 Series Security Features

- Apple ID and Face ID Set-up and Tricks

- Apple Face ID Hidden Features

- All iPhone 8 Gestures you should know

- How to Hide SMS notification content display on iPhone screen

- How to use the virtual Home button

...and a lot more.

There's no better resource around for dummies and seniors such as kids, teens, adolescents, adults, like this guide. It's a must-have manual that every iphone user must-own and also be gifted to friends and family.

It is the complete guide for you, as you would get simplified follow-through instructions on every possible thing you should know about iPhone 8, and iPhone 8 Plus, how you can customize the iPhone as well as amazing Tips & tricks you never would find in the original iPhone manual.

Chapter 1

How to Set up Your brand-new iPhone 8

For many individuals, the iPhone 8 Series would be radically not the same as the previous iPhone model. Not surprisingly, the iPhone set up process hasn't transformed much. However, you might end up on the familiar ground; you may still find a lot of little things you honestly must do before you switch ON your new phone for the very first time (or soon after that).

Let's check out how to set up your brand-new iPhone 8 the proper way.

Setup iPhone 8 the Correct Way

With iPhone 8, you'll have the ability to take benefit of Apple's Automatic Setup. If you're through a mature iPhone without Face Identification, you would see that Touch ID is entirely gone. (Which means you'll save one face, rather than several.)

If you're a serial upgrader, and you're from the year-old iPhone X, less has changed. But you'll still need to update just as usual.

iPhone 8 Set up: The Fundamentals

Re-download only the applications you would need - That one is crucial. Most of us have so many applications on our iPhones that people do not use; this is the big reason we execute a clean set up, in all honesty. Utilize the App Store application and make sure you're authorized into the Apple accounts. (Touch the tiny icon of the Updates -panel to see which accounts you're logged on to.) Only download applications you've found in the past half a year. Or, be daring: download stuff you utilize regularly. We're prepared to wager it'll be considered a very few.

Set up *DO NOT Disturb* - If you're like ordinary people, you're constantly getting notifications, iMessages, and other types of distractions through to your iPhone. Create *DO NOT Disturb* in the Configurations application (it's in the next section listed below, slightly below *Notifications* and *Control Center*). You'll want to routine it for occasions when you need never to be bothered.

Toggle Alarm to On and then Messages when you want

to keep Notifications away from that person. Try 9 p.m. to 8 a.m. when you can.

Pro suggestion: Let some things through if there's an Emergency: Enable Allow Phone calls From your Favorites and toggle Repeated Phone calls to On. iOS 13 also enables you to switch on *DO NOT Disturb* at Bedtime, which mutes all notifications and even hides them from the lock screen, and that means you don't get distracted when you take the phone to check the time.

Auto Setup for iPhone 8

Secondly; Auto Setup enables you to duplicate your Apple ID and home Wi-Fi configurations from another device, simply by getting them close collectively.

In case your old iPhone (or iPad) has already been

operating iOS 12 or iOS 13, to put it simply the devices next to one another. Then follow the prompts to avoid needing to enter your Apple ID and Wi-Fi passwords; this makes the original iPhone set up much smoother.

Set up a fresh iPhone 8 from Scratch

The guide below assumes you're establishing your brand-new iPhone from scratch. If you don't wish to accomplish that, you'll need to acquire any of the other iPhone manuals for beginners that I have written.

Restoring from a back-up of Your old iPhone

It's probably that you'll be restoring your brand-new

iPhone from a back-up of your present iPhone. If that's so, then you merely want to do a couple of things:

- Be sure you come with an up-to-date backup.

- Use Apple's new Auto Setup feature to get you started truly.

The first thing is as simple as going to the iCloud configurations on your iPhone, and looking at that, they're surely is a recent automated back-up. If not, do one by hand. Head to *Configurations > Your Name > iCloud > iCloud Back-up and tap **BACKUP Now***. Wait around until it is done.

Set up Face ID

Face ID is much simpler to use than Touch ID, and it's

own also simpler to create. Instead of needing to teach your iPhone with your fingerprints, one at a time, you simply check out the camera, and that's almost it. To create Face ID on your iPhone, do the next when prompted through the preliminary iPhone setup. (If you'd like to begin over with a phone you set up previously, check out *Settings > Face ID & Passcode, and type in your password, to begin.*)

Establishing Face ID is similar to the compass calibration your iPhone enables you to do from time to time when you use the Maps app. Only rather than rolling the iPhone around, you roll your head. You'll need to do two scans, and then the iPhone 8 would have your 3D head stored in its Secure Enclave, inaccessible to anything - even to iOS itself (despite some clickbait "news" stories).

Now, still, in Settings/*Configurations > Face ID &*

Passcode, you can pick which features to use with Face ID, as everyone else did with *Touch ID*.

If you regularly sport another appearance - you're a clown, a doctor, an impersonator, or something similar - then additionally, you should create another appearance. Just tap the button in the facial ID settings to set this up.

Create iPhone Email

- *Add your email accounts* - Whether you utilize Mail, Perspective, or something similar to Sparrow, you'll want to include your email accounts immediately. For Apple's Email app, touch *Configurations > Accounts & Passwords, then touch Add Accounts*. Choose your email supplier and follow the steps to enter all the knowledge required.

- *See more email preview* - Email lets you start to see the content of a note without starting it. May as well see as a lot of it as you possibly can, right? Utilize Settings > Email and tap on the Preview button. Change your configurations to five lines and get more information from your email messages and never have to get them open up.

- *Established your default accounts* - For reasons unknown, our iOS Email settings always appear to default to a merchant account we never use, like *iCloud.* Tap *Configurations > Accounts & Passwords > Your email accounts name, and then touch Accounts > Email.* Once you reach the depths of the settings, you can touch your preferred email; this would be your address in new mails. (When there is only one address in here, you're all set.) That is also the spot to add some other email addresses associated with your email account.

Advanced iPhone Email tweaks

- *Swipe to control email* - It's much more helpful to have the ability to swipe your email messages away rather than clicking through and tapping on several control keys. Swipe to Archive, so that whenever you swipe that path, you'll have the ability to either quickly save a contact to your Archive. Or, if your email accounts support swiping left as a default Delete action, it'll offer a Garbage icon. Swipe left to Tag as Read, which is a smart way to slam through your electronic mails as you have them. This only impacts your built-in Email application from Apple. Each third-party email customer can do things differently.

- *Add an HTML signature* - A sound email signature really can cause you to look professional, so make sure to include an HTML signature to your email. If you've already got one on the desktop, duplicate and paste the code into contact and ahead to yourself. You'll be able to duplicate and paste it into an Email application (or whichever email supplier you like, if it facilitates it). It could be as easy as textual content formatting tags or as complicated as adding a logo design from a webserver. You should use an iOS application to make one, too; however, they tend to look fairly basic.

Manage Calendars, iCloud, Communications and more

- *Set default Calendar alert times* - Calendar is ideal for alerting you to important occasions, but it's not necessarily at a convenient or useful time. Established the default timing on three types of occasions: Birthdays, Occasions, and All-Day Occasions, and that means you get reminders when they're helpful. Utilize *Configurations > Calendars*. Tap on Default Alert Times and set your Birthday reminders to 1 day before, your Occasions to quarter-hour before (or a period which makes more sense to your mind), and All-Day Occasions on the day of the function (10 a.m.). You'll never miss a meeting again.

- *Background application refresh* - You'll desire to be selective about which applications you desire to be in a position to run in the backdrop, so have a look at the list in *Settings > General > Background App Refresh.* Toggle Background App Refresh to ON, then toggle OFF all the applications you don't need being able to access anything in the background. When in question, toggle it to OFF and find out if you are slowed up by any applications that require to refresh when you release them. You'll want to allow Background Refresh for Cult of Macintosh Magazine!

Secure Your Web Experience

- *Browser set up* - Surfing the net is filled with

forms to complete. Adding your name, address, email, and bank cards may take up a great deal of your power. Make sure to head into Configurations > Browser > AutoFill to create your mobile internet browser the proper way. First, toggle Use Contact Info to On. Then tap on My Info and select the contact you want to use when you encounter form areas in Browser. Toggle Titles and Passwords on as well, and that means you can save that across appointments to the same website. (This pulls from iCloud Keychain, so make sure to have that allowed, too.)

Toggle *CREDIT CARDS* to On as well, which means you can shop swiftly. (be sure to only use SSL-encrypted websites.)

Pro suggestion: Manage which bank cards your iPhone

helps you to save with a tap on BANK CARDS. You can include new cards within, or delete ones that no more work or that you don't want to use via mobile Browser.

The browser in iOS 13 and later version also blocks cross-site monitoring, which are those cookies that follow you around and let online stores place the same advertisements on every subsequent web page you visit. That is On by default, and that means you should not do anything. Just relax and revel in your newfound personal privacy.

iCloud Everywhere

- *iCloud is everything* - There's without a doubt in our thoughts that iCloud is the easiest, optimum solution for keeping all of your stuff supported and safe. Utilize the Configurations > iCloud and be sure to register with your **Apple ID**. You can manage your storage space in here, but make sure to enable all you need immediately. Enable iCloud Drive, Photos, Connections, Reminders, Browser, Records, News, Wallet, Back-up, Keychain and others once you get the iPhone unpacked. You can enable Email and Calendars if you merely use Apple's applications and services; usually, you would keep those toggled OFF.

Services subscription during iPhone setup

- *Enable iCloud Photo Library* - We love the iCloud Photo Library. It maintains your photos and videos securely stored in the cloud and enable you to get full-quality copies of your documents in the event you misplace your originals. iCloud Picture Library depends on your iCloud storage space, if you have many photos, you'll want to bump that up. Utilize Configurations > iCloud > Photos, then toggle iCloud Image Library to On. (Remember that this will switch off My Picture Stream. If you'd like both, you'll need to re-toggle Image Stream back again to On.)

- *Use iTunes Match* - Sure, Apple Music monitors all the music data files on your devices, but if you delete them from your iPhone and don't have a back-up elsewhere, you're heading to have to stay for whatever quality Apple Music will provide you with when you listen. If you wish to maintain your full-resolution music documents supported to the cloud, use iTunes Match. You get all of your music files matched up or published to iCloud in the best bitrate possible. After that, you can stream or download the music to any device provided your iTunes Match membership is intact. Never be without your music (or have an over-filled iPhone) again. Go to *Configurations* > *Music*. Then touch on Sign up to iTunes Match to understand this valuable service allowed on your brand-new iPhone.

More iPhone set up Tweaks

- ***Extend your Auto-Lock*** - Let's face it. The default two minutes you get for the Volume of time your iPhone would remain on without turning off its screen may keep the battery higher much longer, but it's insufficient for anybody during regular use. Utilize Configurations, General, Auto-Lock to create this to the whole five minutes, which means you can stop tapping your screen at all times to keep it awake.

- *Get texts everywhere* - You can enable your Mac PC or iPad to get texts from your iPhone, provided you've set up iMessage to them (Settings, Text messages, toggle iMessage to ON on any iOS device, Messages Preferences on your Mac). Ensure that your other device is close by when you utilize Settings on your iPhone, then touch Messages > TEXT Forwarding. Any devices available will arrive on the list. Toggle your Mac or iPad to On, and then check the prospective device for a code. Enter that code into your iPhone. Now all of your devices are certain to get not only iMessages but also texts from those not using iMessage.

- *Equalize your tunes* - Start the EQ in your Music

application to be able to hear your preferred jams and never have a trouble with a bluetooth speaker. Go to Configurations > Music. Once there, touch on EQ and established your iPhone to NIGHT TIME; this will provide you with a great quantity raise for those times where you want to blast *The Clash* while you make a quick supper in the kitchen.

Chapter 2

iPhone 8 Unique Beginners Tips

We know thousands of individuals just obtained an iPhone 8 when relatives and buddies members upgraded to one of Apple's newer models, so if you're left with one, here are some iPhone 8/8 Plus changes that may not be familiar to you.

(If you've never used iOS 12 before, then you'll find a lot more improvements, but these improvements will be the ones unique to iPhone 8 compared to previous models - but do take a peek through my other hints for some ideas to get more from your brand-new device).

How to Reboot your iPhone

If you've used a youthful model iPhone before getting an

iPhone 8, then you should know that Apple has changed how you Force Restart the unit.

Using the iPhone 8, the Force Restart procedure is really as follows:

- Press and quickly release the *Volume Up* button.

- Immediately press the *Volume Down* button.

- Then press the *Sleep/Wake button* until you start to see the Apple logo.

How to update the software

You should upgrade the program whenever a new version comes, but if you come with an iPhone 8 (or 8 Plus) you will probably still be in a position to upgrade its software in 2022.

How to utilize it one-handed

This won't take long. Keep your iPhone and double-tap the *Home button* to bring your windows down the display screen (you'll know it when you view it) to make things simpler to reach with your thumb. Double-tap again to move it up. And, if you will be keying in one-handed, reach over and press 'n' contain the emoji button the keypad .. on another web page you'll find three keyboards, right, middle and left. Choose the best hand indent if you work with your left hands and the keypad will twist to the left to make it just a little more straightforward to use.

How to charge your iPhone 8 faster

iPhone 8 boasts with a 5-watt charger, but when you can obtain an iPad Pro or USB-C MacBook charger, you can plug your device into those. You'll notice a real improvement in control time when you do. You should strike 50% charge in thirty minutes utilizing a 29W MacBook charger. You can even charge your device wirelessly utilizing a *Qi charger* (nevertheless, you probably understood that).

How to use the improved Family Portrait Mode

If you've used an iPhone 7, you'll know just a little about Family portrait Mode, which gets better still in the XS devices but continues to be great in 8. Family portrait mode was launched with the iPhone 7 Plus, and in iPhone 8 Plus has got the new capability to enable you to change the light effect you utilize once you take the shot.

Just open a Family portrait shot in Photos, tap *Edit* and use it as an editing effect. Family portrait mode requires (as the name suggests) better family portrait shots. You can even play with different Family portrait Lighting configurations while taking your shot. (To eliminate the Depth impact, open up the image in Photos in Edit setting and touch the Depth button.)

How to use the Trick cursor

If you are typing or wanting to choose words in editable text, touch, and hang on the keyboard, and you'll suddenly see it has become a cursor to make it much simpler to select words you will need.

Ways to get better Video

Your iPhone 8 catches the video at 4K quality at 30 fps by default. That's very good quality and should look great, but you can get even higher quality video (though be careful not to fill up your phone with clips you don't need). *Open Settings> Camera> Record Video*, and you may choose to capture your clips at 4K res and a speedy 60fps.

How to handle True Tone

iPhone 8 devices were the first ever to provide True Tone displays. These use light sensors to dynamically change the colour of the display to higher match room lighting, so the colors of what you are looking at on-screen appear to be more consistent; this isn't always what you want, so you can turn this feature off in Control Center by long-pressing the iPhone Brightness button and then switching True Tone off (or on). You can also disable it in *Settings> Display & Brightness>* toggle it to off.

How to use Slow Sync

iPhone 8 series devices were the first ever to support

Slow Sync, a technology that tries to mitigate the distraction of taking a graphic using the flash and also attempts to lessen that weird effect that makes the primary item in your image appear all bleached out while the background to look darker.

This feature functions by slowing the shutter speed while making the flash moment faster; this implies the backdrop should look brighter and the adobe flash distraction should be reduced.

The result? Better photos when working with display, even of moving items. What you ought to do? Nothing at all, it's built-in.

Chapter 3

iPhone 8 - Top Features

After months of rumors, leaking, and lots of speculation, the iPhone 8 has finally been unveiled. This latest flagship smartphone as of 2017 was proven to the world throughout a major keynote at Apple's new HQ in Cupertino the other day. The iPhone 8 and much larger iPhone 8 Plus both add several improvements over their predecessors making them the best Apple smartphones as at now.

Alongside the iPhone 8, the united states technology also largely revealed its iPhone X that includes a new design with a display that covers the whole front of these devices. However, with a £999 price, and a release time of November 2018, the iPhone X would be out.

1. Wireless Charging

Apple has included wifi charging on its latest smartphone; this means it can get a fill-up by merely being placed on the compatible pad. The iPhone 8 uses the established Qi ecosystem this means it will use most accessories available on the marketplace.

It's well worth noting that Apple doesn't add a charging pad in the package, so you should buy one separately to utilize this new feature. As well as wireless charging, the iPhone 8 can have its battery boosted in super-quick time. A fresh Apple-designed image signal processor provides advanced pixel processing, wide colour capture, faster autofocus in low light and better HDR photos, while a fresh quad-LED True Tone Flash with Decrease Sync leads to more uniformly lit backgrounds and foregrounds.

Apple says that this results in outstanding photos with vibrant, realistic colors and greater detail. The iPhone 8 Plus retains its dual-lens camera, which, along using its smart zoom and Family portrait Mode, is now able to change the light in pictures.

Portrait Light brings dramatic studio room lights to the iPhone, allowing customers to fully capture stunning portraits with a shallow depth-of-field impact in five different light styles.

2. *A11 Bionic Processor*

Apple's boosting its new processor chip is the quickest ever to be observed within an iPhone. The brand new *A11 Bionic chip* has around 30% faster graphics performance than the prior brains found inside the iPhone 7. If true it's more likely to outperform not only its predecessor but all the latest Google android competition in year 2017 ans early 2018.

3. *New Colors & Cup Design*

Apple has included some new colours on the iPhone 8 with these devices happening sale in space grey, gold, and silver. The iPhone 8 and iPhone 8 Plus also introduce a lovely cup back design and do not worry about any of it breaking as Apple says it is the most durable cup ever in a smartphone.

The finish is manufactured utilizing a seven-layer colour process for precise hue and opacity, delivering a rich depth of colour with a colour-matched aerospace-grade aluminum bezel. Both iPhone 8 and iPhone 8 Plus are also water and dust resistant.

4. *Extra Storage*

There's some good news if you are always working out

of space for storage as Apple has included 64GB as standard. That is double the essential memory on the iPhone 7. Apple, in addition, has ditched the 128GB version with the iPhone 8 featuring 256GB of in-built memory space.

It's also worthy of noting that iOS 11, which launches in a few days, will automatically decrease the size of photos taken on the iPhone's camera, providing users even more extra space.

5 Cool iPhone 8 Features

1. AR - Augmented Reality

This essentially the most impressive new feature of the iPhone 8 because of its ability to perform augmented reality (AR) apps. They don't need multiple digital cameras or sensors to operate. AR applications simply rely on the iPhone 8's back camera.

Since AR technology continues to be relatively new rather than so trusted, the amount of applications using AR is continually increasing. AR offers a new way for individuals to play video games, learn, and shop. It's also useful in everyday living: you may use AR to, for example, measure things easily without a tape measure.

The world-famous furniture merchant IKEA, in addition, has launched its AR app. IKEA Place provides 3D types of IKEA furniture and allows an individual to put them in real-world environments; This implies you don't have to buy a couch or seat and transport to your living room to see whether it suits or not. You can merely use the IKEA application to learn. The application also allows users to buy and order products.

2. Powerful Picture Editing

The iPhone 8 features Apple's powerful new A11 Bionic processor and a better camera. These characteristics make the iPhone 8 a great tool even for professional photographers. The App Store has a great assortment of picture editing apps. Using the right apps, you may make your photos look superb and professional. Among my favourites is **Photofox**. It combines the simpleness of mobile editing and enhancing with the energy and countless top features of desktop apps, such as *Adobe Photoshop.*

The app helps you to edit images in levels, which can be an important function in professional picture editing. Creating unique designs with visual elements is uncomplicated and straightforward. The application is free but contains in-app purchases.

3. 4K Video

The iPhone 8's camera has become powerful smartphone cameras in the marketplace. Among its most exceptional features is its capability to take 4K video at 60 fps. What's more, the iPhone 8 can also record excellent gradual movement video at 240 fps with 1080p resolution. If you wish to customise your iPhone's camera configurations, go to *Settings > Camera.*

4. Portraits with Portrait Lighting

Apple introduced the astonishing Family portrait photo setting in the iPhone 7 Plus. The iPhone 8 Plus will take things to another level with Family portrait Lighting.

In brief, Family portrait photo mode gives you razor-sharp portrait photos of your subject matter with a blurry background. The iPhone 8 Plus, however, provides you the choice of adding special lights like in real a studio room. The very best part is that once you've taken a picture using Portrait mode, you can still change the lighting settings afterwards to make your picture look the same as you want to buy too.

You can customise the light settings of the portrait picture you already took simply by tapping *Edit* on the picture in the Photos app. The Family portrait Lighting wheel should come up, which you can slide to change the image configurations.

5. Screen Recording

The brand new iPhones include native screen recording built-in - there's no dependence on third-party apps; this new feature comes in the iPhone's Control Centre, which you can access by swiping up from underneath the screen.

The display documenting icon is not in the Control Centre by default; you will need to add it by heading to the iPhone's configurations/settings page.

Chapter 4

19 Essential iPhone 8 Guideline Tips

It's a shame the iPhone 8 and iPhone 8 Plus didn't include new designs because while they appear to be a somewhat different iPhone 7 and iPhone 7 Plus, there are a few massive improvements under the hood: ridiculously fast processors, better still cameras plus some brilliant new features.

And here we present 19 ways to make your iPhone 8 / 8 Plus experience better still through an array of different tips, methods, and useful alternatives to the things you need to do every day with your handset - use these to become power consumers of your brand-new Apple phone.

1. *Press the keyboard*

The iPhone 8 is big, and the iPhone 8 Plus bigger still. If you're battling to type one-handed, press, and contain the emoji button on the keypad, and you'll see three keypad symbols: a left-hand part keypad, the existing standard keypad, and a right-hand aspect keypad. Choose either left or to squish the keypad to that part for easier keying in.

2. *Customize Control Center*

The redesigned Control Center is a lot handier than before, and you may make it handier by changing its material in *Settings > Control Center > Customize Settings*. You'll find some interesting options within, like the option to include screen documenting or control your Apple Television.

3. *Drag and Drop*

iPhones haven't yet got the energy to drag and drop between apps, nevertheless, you can now drag and drop inside Apple's applications - and that means you can drag a connection in an Email into a fresh message, move text in one Note to some other, etc. In Records, for example, you work in scenery mode and drag a graphic or textual content selection out, and on the notice you want to drop it into; after that get note opens, and you will move your stop of textual content or image to its desired location. In the Documents application you can move items over folders to move them.

4. *Check out QR codes*

Apple is very late to the QR code party; nevertheless, you can now check out QR rules from within the Camera app. It'll automatically notice that it's taking a look at a QR code and can then allow you to open up the hyperlink in

Safari, hook up to the Wi-Fi network, or do other things the code was created to do.

5. *Make Communications Messier, or Mute them*

You will find new effects in Messages: to see them, hold down the Send icon, and tap Screen. You can mute discussions in Communications now too: swipe still left on a discussion and tap Cover Alerts.

6. *Loop Your Live Photos*

Live Photos are lots of fun, and they're even more pleasurable on the iPhone 8 and iPhone 8 Plus: swipe the picture up to start to see the effects options, which allow you to loop or bounce your Live Photo, or apply a long-exposure effect.

7. *A Record at any Resolution*

The camera in the iPhone 8 and 8 Plus shoots 4K at 30 fps by default, nevertheless, you can modify that in *Settings > Camera > Record Video* to improve the speed to 60fps, drop it to 24fps or use a lesser resolution such as 1080p or 720p HD. Normally, the bigger the quality and framework rate, the greater space you'll need to store your video.

8. *Charge without Cables*

You might have seen that both iPhone 8 and the iPhone 8 Plus support the Qi charging standard, so they'll use any Qi-compatible pad, like the pads and charging-enabled furniture IKEA offers. You can even buy an Apple-approved charging pad from Mophie or Belkin for $59.95 / £54.95 / AU$99.95, with Apple's own AirPower pad coming later this season. It's less fast as charging with a wire, but it's much more convenient and Apple reckons it isn't remote in conditions of speed.

9. *Change Light in Family Portrait Mode*

This only is a plus, and it's one of the headlines top features of the phone. Family portrait setting has new light options that allow you to choose from different studio room light and stage lights, and the email address details are instant - there's some serious digestion making the magic happen so quickly, and the initial data is kept so you can transform your brain later.

10. *Uncover the Power of Sluggish Sync*

Photo benefits will find out about slow sync adobe flash already because it's something many digital cameras can do - it's a means to getting more balanced photos when using display in low light by keeping the shutter open up for longer.

In a standard flash photo, the subject is brightly lit and the background dark, but with decrease sync it's much nearer to what you observe with your eye. You don't should do anything to allow this program - it's just area of the camera.

11. *Enter AR*

The iPhone 8 and 8 Plus cameras have been created for augmented reality (AR) applications because of the high power of the A11 Bionic chip. Yes, other cell phones in the number can do the same, but you will get the best experience on the latest handsets. It's lots of fun, and a thrilling glimpse into the future, whether you are looking at IKEA furniture overlaid on your living room or Thomas & Friends Minis on the espresso table.

12. *Change the Picture Format*

iOS 11 introduced a fresh, a lot more efficient extendable

for photos called HEIF, and it's the default format. However, if you would like to store photos in the less effective but more broadly backed JPEG format, you can transform the default in *Configurations > Camera > Types*.

You can do the same with video, changing from HEVC to H.264 as the default. Don't be concerned about carrying this out if you want to talk about the odd picture. When you talk about iOS, it automatically changes from the high-efficiency format to JPEG or H.264.

13. *Share Your Storage*

This is a large one for families: now you can share your iCloud space with the family. for example, we've got a 2TB plan that people share with the youngsters. You can allow this in *Settings > iCloud > Manage Storage*.

Don't get worried; your key iCloud documents aren't distributed, just your space for storage.

14. *Don't Crash the Automobile*

Using your telephone while travelling is, of course, stupid and dangerous, but if you're uncertain that you can avoid temptation then allow *DO NOT Disturb* While Traveling in *Settings* > *DO NOT Disturb*.

The name lets you know what it can, however, not how clever it is: your iPhone can tell how fast you're moving or whether you're linked for an in-car Bluetooth system, and turn the feature on automatically. It won't stop phone calls, and folks can still reach you within an emergency. However, be warned! It'll also do the same on the train, which may be irritating on the commute to work and you're sitting thinking why nobody enjoys you.

15. *Organize Your Files*

The brand new Files app is currently on iPhone, and it's a useful way of accessing not only iCloud but third-party services such as Dropbox and Google Drive too. However, most file exchanges are still dealt with by the inbuilt 'Talk about' icon in the relevant apps, rather than using Data files, but if you would like to talk about things from Webpages or similar, this is the spot to come.

16. *Toggle True Tone*

The iPhone 8 and 8 Plus get a good feature that once was limited to iPads: True Tone screen, which adjusts the screen color temperature and brightness predicated on the ambient light conditions. In the unlikely event that you don't want the colors to become more realistic on the display screen, you can toggle it in *Settings > Display and Brightness* or by pressing hard on the brightness slider in charge Center, through 3D Touch.

17. Switch off Auto-Brightness

If you like to adapt to the display's brightness yourself rather than leaving it to your iPhone's care setting, you'll wish to know the new location of Auto-Brightness - it's been moved out of *Settings > Display & Brightness and today live in Settings > Accessibility > Display Accommodations.*

18. Plan Emergencies

The brand new Emergency SOS feature, which you can allow in *Settings > Emergency SOS*, disables **Touch ID** when activated and can automatically call an emergency number or notify named contacts that you'll require assistance. To utilize it, ***press the Power Button five(5) times***.

19. Get Yourself a Guide

I have written a lot of books on how to use several iPhone devices, the titps and tricks needed, ipad guide books and lot more. Many Authors under Engolee Publishing House has written other Guide too. Also; Apple has published a huge iPhone consumer guide for iBooks. It's free, and you could obtain it for additional information.

Chapter 5

Using iPhone 8 without Home Button

Gestures on the iPhone's touchscreen will always be important, but without the Home button the iPhone 8 and later models, gestures become essential. To execute functions just like a turn off or time for the Home screen on your iPhone 8, iPhone 8 plus, you are going to use unique gestures that combine the medial side and Volume control keys instead of the lacking Home button. Common features, like speaking with Siri, starting Apple Pay, and shutting apps, will have unique gestures that utilize your phone's physical control keys, Face ID, and the touchscreen. This chapter addresses all the tips you should know, like how to use Reachability, have a screenshot, as well as how to briefly disable Face ID the iPhone 8, iPhone 8 plus. Let's get started doing how to use gestures to get around iPhone models 8 and later.

There are a significant number of new gestures and changes to navigate the iPhone, given that Apple did away with the Home button. You're probably acquainted with the most common iPhone gestures, such as pinching with two fingertips to focus or Tremble to Undo. You can also pull multiple photos and drop them into another app. Gestures on the iPhone would always be an integral part of the routine. However, the iPhone 8 launched a lot of new ways to do old stuff. Unless in any other case, indicated these procedures all connect with the iPhone 8,iPhone 11, iPhone 11 Pro, and iPhone 11 Pro Max.

How to Unlock Your iPhone with Raise to Wake

Raise to Wake is fired up by default on the iPhone 8 and other newer models. To use *Raise to Wake* on the iPhone 8, iPhone 8 plus, lift your iPhone, and the screen would automatically start. If *Raise to Wake* isn't working, likely, you have accidentally handicapped the feature inside Configurations.

How to Enable Raise to Wake:

- Open up the *Settings* app.

- Select *Screen & Brightness.*

- Toggle Raise to Wake to the ON position to allow the feature.

You don't need to lift your phone awaken the screen on iPhone 8; you can merely touch the screen to awaken your iPhone 8, even if Raise to Wake is impaired.

How to Unlock the iPhone 8 & Newer iPhones

To unlock your iPhone 8, iPhone 8 plus, or iPhone 11, you would need to ensure that a Face ID is established. Using Face ID, you can boost or tap your iPhone 8, or other newer models, to wake and unlock your iPhone by looking straight at the screen.

How exactly to Unlock an iPhone 8 or Later Using Face ID:

- Wake the screen up by either tapping the screen or using Raise to Wake.

- Look directly at the screen to use Face ID to unlock your device.

- Swipe up from underneath of your Lock screen to visit the Home screen.

- If, for just about any reason, Face ID didn't unlock your mobile phone, swipe up from underneath of the screen to retry Face ID or even to enter your passcode instead. Once you have input your passcode, your iPhone will automatically go back to the Home screen, or whatever application was open up last.

How to Open up the Control & Notification Centers

The notch on the iPhone 8 and later models divide the very best of the screen into a left and right hands screen.

On your own iPhone 8, iPhone 8 plus, the right part of the notch near the top of the screen is used to gain access to your Control Center while the left side is utilized to open up Notifications.

- To open Control Center, swipe down from the right-hand side of the screen.

- To open Notifications, swipe down from the left-hand side of the screen.

How to Go back to the Home screen From an App

Returning to the home screen can appear impossible if there is no Home button. Around the iPhone 8, iPhone 8 plus, and 11, you can go back to your home screen by following the instructions below.

How to Go back to the Home Screen:

- From within any app, place your finger on the home bar underneath the centre of the screen.

- Swipe up toward the very top of your screen.

How to Activate Apple Pay

On previous iPhone models, twice tapping the home button raised Apple Pay from a locked screen, but on the iPhone 8 or later you will have to use a fresh gesture to gain access to **Apple Pay**. To use Apple Pay from a locked screen on the iPhone 8, iPhone 8 plus, you will have to double click your side button and use Face ID to continue with Apple Pay. Here's how to use Apple Pay on iPhones without a Home button:

- Double click on the Part button to open up Apple Pay

- Look into your iPhone screen to verify with Face ID.

If Apple Pay doesn't appear when the medial side button is double-clicked, 1 of 2 things is undoubtedly going on: either you haven't created a debit card with Apple Pay (check even though you have; my cards disappeared after establishing my new iPhone) or you do not have Apple Pay allowed in settings; this is fixed with the next steps:

- Open up the Settings app.

- Select Face ID & Passcode.

- Toggle ON **Apple Pay** under Use **Face ID** For.

How to Power Off the iPhone 8

Sometimes, you will need to power your iPhone off for a movie, a lecture, or other events that want your full attention. Like previous models, whenever your iPhone 8, iPhone 8 plus, are a runoff, then you will have to use a gesture to turn your iPhone back On carefully.

To carefully *Turn On* the iPhone 8 or later models, press and maintain the side button before the Apple logo design appears.

How to Access Siri with side Button

Removing the home button also changes how you access Siri on the iPhone 8 and newer models.

- If you wish to use gestures rather than Hey Siri on

the iPhone 8, iPhone 8 plus, then you will have to use the medial side button to gain access to Siri.

- Click and hold the Side button (formerly known as the Rest/Wake button) to speak to Siri.

How to Take Screenshots without the home Button

Sometimes, you would need to have a screenshot to save lots of a great formula as a graphic or to keep hold of a text to examine later.

- To have a screenshot on the iPhone 8, iPhone 8 plus, you'll use a mixture of the medial side and volume buttons rather than utilizing a Home button.

- To consider screenshot on your iPhone 8, or a later model iPhone, concurrently press and release the medial side button and Volume Up button.

How to Enable & Activate Reachability

Reachability slashes off the low fifty percent of the screen and moves the very best part of your screen to underneath, making it simpler to reach the very best of your screen with one hand. By default, Reachability has switched off on the iPhone X, XS, XS Max, and 11; nevertheless, you can allow the Reachability feature inside the Settings portion of your Configurations app.

To allow Reachability on your iPhone 8, iPhone 11, 11 Pro, and 11 Pro Max:

- Open up the *Settings* app.

- Select *General.*

- Touch *Accessibility.*

- Toggle on *Reachability.*

- Swipe down on the home bar or bottom level middle of the screen to activate Reachability.

Given that you've allowed Reachability, you can activate the feature within any application by swiping down on the horizontal part, also called the home feature, at the bottom of your screen. There is no home pub on the home screen; nevertheless, you can still activate Reachability on the home screen by swiping down from underneath the middle of the screen where you'll typically find the home feature.

How to Change Between & Force Quit Apps

You would find two various ways to change between applications on the iPhone 8: with the App Switcher and without. You can gain access to the App Switcher on the iPhone 8, iPhone 8 plus, by partly swiping upwards from underneath the screen. You can even switch between applications by swiping the home bar still left or right.

How to Open up the App Switcher on the iPhone 8, iPhone 8 plus:

- Swipe halfway up from underneath the screen.

- Lift your finger, and the App Switcher would open up. You can swipe through, much like previous models, and touch on an application to open up it.

- To eliminate an application from App Switcher, swipe through to the app.

To switch applications without starting the App Switcher:

- Place your finger on the home bar or underneath the middle of the screen if the home button is absent.

- Swipe from left to open up your latest applications in descending order.

How to Switch OFF Power & Perform a hard Restart

The Home button was central to numerous functions, including powering down your iPhone or forcing a hard restart whenever your iPhone freeze. To power down or push a hard restart on the iPhone 8, iPhone 11 Pro, and 11 Pro Max, you would have to perform new gestures that involve a mixture of the medial side and Volume Up buttons.

To turn from the iPhone 8, iPhone 8 plus:

- Hold down the medial side button and the Volume Up or Down button before the option to slip to power off shows up.

- Using the Slip to Force Off toggle, swipe to the right.

You can even switch off the iPhone 8, iPhone 8 plus from the overall portion of the Settings app.

- Open up the Settings application and choose *General*.

- scroll completely down to underneath, and tap TURN OFF.

- Glide to power icon to turn the power off.

You are capable of doing a hard restart, sometimes called a force shutdown, on your iPhone 8, iPhone 8 plus. To execute a hard restart:

- Quickly press and release the Volume Up

accompanied by the Volume Down button.

- Now, press and maintain the side button before the device shuts down, and the Apple logo design appears.

- Your iPhone would automatically restart.

It's good to notice that whenever performing a hard Restart, it requires the iPhone 8 a couple of seconds to turn off when you're pressing the medial side button. So don't quit! I thought it wasn't working initially, but I needed to sustain the side button pressed down for a longer length of time.

How to Temporarily Disable Face ID

Face ID is not a perfect system; users have reported that some family members have had the opportunity to use cell phones protected Face ID due to a strong family resemblance. To briefly disable Face ID, you would have to keep down the medial side and Volume Up control keys to talk about the turn off-screen, and then tap Cancel to Force your iPhone to require the passcode to unlock briefly.

Here's how to briefly disable *Face ID* on the iPhone 8, iPhone 8 plus:

- Hold down the Volume Up or Down button and the medial side button simultaneously.

- After the shutdown screen appears, forget about the buttons. That is important; if you keep up to carry down the control keys, Emergency SOS would automatically be brought on.

- Touch the X at the bottom to cancel the shutdown.

Now, Face ID is briefly handicapped until you enter your passcode. Once you enter your passcode, Face ID would continue working as typical.

Chapter 6

How to Fix Common iPhone 8 Problems

If you own an iPhone 8, you might come across occasional issues like display screen freezing, problems with contacts, or overheating. Luckily, these common iPhone 8 issues have easy solutions to get your iPhone 8 back again to performing as it will.

How to Fix the most frequent iPhone 8 Problems

- *Soft or Hard Reset your iPhone*: You might sometimes find your iPhone's display either trapped in a scenery orientation or just frozen. Usually, this is solved with a smooth reset, but if it doesn't handle it, get one of these hard reset. After the iPhone restarts, the display screen should be back again to normal.

- *Ensure that your telephone is operating the latest version of iOS*: If it is not, upgrade it immediately, as a revise may contain necessary software and bug fixes.

- *Update apps*: One of the most frustrating mistakes that can occur when working with your iPhone is having an application quit in the middle of an important task. Check the App Store and install any improvements for the application involved; try uninstalling and reinstalling the application to find out if it begins working again. You can even try contacting the application programmer to see if they're aware of the problem.

- *Reset Bluetooth*: Bluetooth loudspeakers and

earphones are something essential for iPhone 8 users because the device does not have a 3.5mm headphone jack port. However, there were some issues reported in linking wireless earphones and other Bluetooth devices. If you still have issues hooking up with a specific Bluetooth device, you may want to try syncing a different device.

- *Reconnect to Wi-Fi or refresh your network configurations:* Sometimes iPhone 8 users statement Wi-Fi issues, including sluggish rates of speed, erroneously getting a "wrong security password" message, or difficulty linking to a network whatsoever. Ensure your web connection and router are fired up and working properly, as well.

- One of the most commonly reported problems with

the iPhone 8 has been these devices overheating while utilizing a demanding program or game. Thankfully, you'll find so many ways to handle this particular concern, from disabling certain background features, to eliminating the situation by deleting battery-intensive apps.

- Avoid departing your iPhone in sunlight or close to any heating system elements, like heaters or computer vents.

- If you experience problems with 3D Touch shortcuts showing up or moving prematurely that you should access, you can optimize the 3D Touch level of sensitivity as needed.

- *Reset All Settings:* While this may cause you to reduce any preserved Wi-Fi passwords, it can benefit to fix various problems. To get this done, tap *Configurations > General > Reset > Reset All Configurations.*

- Make certain Apple services will work by heading to Apple's website and looking into the status. If you suddenly end up unable to hook up to the Apple App Store on your iPhone, this is the very first thing you should check. Change your iPhone's LTE settings to Data Only. In case your iPhone phone calls are filled up with static, and there is certainly difficulty making out what your partner is saying, faucet Configurations > Cellular Data > Cellular Data Options > Enable LTE > Data Only. Change LTE back on after looking at your connection quality, if needed.

Chapter 7

23 Key iPhone Tips and Hacks You Should Know

Sure, there's a lot your trusty iPhone can already do, even if you have not upgraded to the shiny new iPhone 11 Pro Max yet. At a pinch, you could probably serve small canapés off it. But this pocketable package of question isn't only a fairly vessel in to the world of internet pleasure and messaging madness.

There are a large number of cool iPhone features hidden under the surface that you almost certainly weren't even alert to - and not only the data that can litter may bring your phone back from a watery death.

They are among the better iPhone hacks you didn't find out about, and just how you will get them.

1. *Charge Your Phone Faster with an Individual*

Button Press

Tired of looking forward to your phone to recharge? Well, there's a way to increase the re-juicing process, and it's remarkably simple. Apply Flight Safe setting. By knocking out all of your phone's Wi-Fi-searching, data-draining communication, it requires any risk of straining off your electric battery strength while it's being driven up. Not greatly true, but if you are pressed for time and seeking to take out of the juice, that extra 4% you'll add 30 minutes linked to the mains will make all the difference.

2. Shave Seconds Off Your Searches

With regards to learning the footy ratings or proving a spot, getting where you will need to be on the internet is focused on speed and precision, something is missing if you are forced to knock out type-heavy websites. To save time by keeping down the entire stop icon while keying in and out an address to talk about a short-cut group of URL suffixes. From your classics (.com, .co.uk) to the less used (.edu, .ie), there are quick-strike shortcuts for all those.

3. *Discover just what Your Mobile Phone is Aware of*

Somewhat sinisterly, your iPhone is always gathering data for you in the background - whether it is the applications you're using the most, how much data you're churning through, or even, most creepily, what your location is. To see what we should mean, check out *Settings > Personal privacy > Location Services > System Services > Regular Locations.* Here you can view not merely where you've been, but how long you've spent in each place.

4. *Replace a Toolbox Essential*

You've probably submitted away the Compass application alongside the Shares and discover Friends applications in a folder entitled *'Crap I cannot delete'*. You should draw it out again, as it offers a key second function that will assist with your DIY responsibilities. Instead, swiping the left in the Compass application brings up an extremely useful soul level - an electronic bubble measure than can check if that shelf is really level.

5. *Lock Your Camera's Center Point*

Everybody knows that tapping the display while going for a picture will set the camera's point of concentration, right? Good. Annoyingly though, each time you move the camera after deciding on a centre point, it disappears. Rather than just tapping the display screen, press for another or two until an *'AF Locked'* container pops up. You will twist, change and swing finished around without dropping focus.

6. *Create Custom Vibrations*

Ever wished you could show who's calling simply by how your telephone feels buzzing against your lower-leg? You will: In Connections, select your person of preference and strike *Edit*. Here you will see a Vibration option. Selecting this will provide you with a lot of options, like the **Create New Vibration** tool. Making your bespoke hype is really as simple as tapping the display to the defeat of your decision.

7. *Correct Siri's Pronunciation*

Siri's a little of the smug know-it-all - so there is nothing better than getting in touch with it on its dick ups. Like when it mispronounces individuals' names as an ignorant Brit overseas. So if Siri says something amiss, inform it. Pursuing up a blunder by stating "That isn't how you pronounce..." you will discover Siri require the right pronunciation that enables you to check it offers things right. Because everybody knows it's Levi-O-sa, not Levi-o-SAR.

8. *Close 3 Apps Simultaneously*

It's not simply pictures and webpages that support multi-finger gestures. You can toss additional digits into unscrambling your iPhone mess too. If you want to shut multiple applications in a rush for totally innocent, not concealing anything, honest reasons - you can pull three fingers through to the multitasking menu to cull the mess quickly; this means your mobile phone should be snappier in double-quick time.

9. *Manage Your Music on the Timer*

Enjoy hearing just little soothing vocals as you drift off to the Land of Nod? Then you're probably all too acquainted with getting up at 3 am for some unwanted music. Unless, of course, you arranged your music to turn off on the timer carefully. In the Clock app, slip along to the Timer options. Hereunder the 'When Time

Ends' label, you can replace the security alarm option for a 'Stop Playing' label; this will switch off the music, whether it is through Apple Music or Spotify when the timer strikes zero.

10. *Have a Photo without coming in contact with Your Phone*

An oldie but a goodie iPhone hack is making use of your volume control buttons to fully capture simple, thus keeping your meaty paw blocking the display screen as you try to strike the touchscreen settings. But if you like to be even more taken off your photo-capturing shutter handles, Hitting the volume button on a set of compatible, connected earphones will have the same impact.

11. *Save Your Valuable Data Allowance by Restricting App Access*

You're only a third of just halfway through the month, as

well as your 2GB data allowance has already been beginning to look just a little extended. You don't need to scale back on your on-the-go Netflix looking. Instead, go for which applications get demoted to the Wi-Fi-only B-list. Head to Configurations > Mobile Data where you may make the best decisions one application at the same time.

12. *Improve Your Electric Battery Life*

Limelight, Apple's linked quick-access for key data and services, is ideal for offering access immediately to the latest breaking information, sports ratings and social upgrade. But very much stuff happening in the background can eat your electric battery life whole. If you don't turn off Limelight features for several applications to take out more life per charge, that is. Just go *Configurations > General > Limelight Search* and limit what's attracting data behind your consent.

13. *Improve Your Transmission by Knowing Where You Can Search For It*

You don't need to go out of initial floor windows trying to find where your iPhone's connection is most beneficial. Type *3001#12345#* into the iPhone's dialler and strike call to release the concealed Field Setting tool. This sub-surface menu becomes your pub chart-based signal indication into an even more simple numerical-based sign signifier. Got a rating of -50? Then you will be enjoying Hd-video streams on the road. Down around -120, though, and you will battle to send a textual content. Just follow the figures to better indicators.

14. *Find out Just How Long You've been Looking Forward To A Reply*

We've all been there: endlessly rechecking our cell phones for a textual content reply, thinking how long it has been since we sent our message of love. There's a simple way to learn, though swipe in from the right-hand part of the display when in a messaging thread, showing exact delivery times for each message delivered and received. True, it isn't as morale-beating as WhatsApp's blue ticks, but it'll still offer you a complicated over why it's overtaking 42 minutes for your other fifty percent to reply. Do affairs take that long?

15. *Share Your Loved Ones Tree with Siri*

Does discussing your parents by their given name cause you to feel awkward? Then train Siri to learn whom you're chatting with. Ask Siri to call your father, and the digital PA should ask who your dad is. Once a contact has been designated to the parental moniker, each time you require pops continue, you'll be supported by simple, fuss-free phoning.

Chapter 8

How to Customize Your iPhone Mobile

Customize iPhone Ringtones & Text message Tones

The ringtones and text tones your iPhone uses to get your attention need not be exactly like everyone else's. You may make all types of changes, including changing the tone, and that means you know who's phoning or texting without even taking a glance at your phone.

- ***Change the Default Ringtone***: Your iPhone comes pre-loaded with a large number of ringtones. Change the default ringtone for all those calls to the main one you prefer the better to get notified when you experience a call to arrive. Do this by *heading to Settings -> Noises (Noises & Haptics on some models) -> Ringtone.*

- *Set Person Ringtones*: You can assign a different ringtone for everybody in your connections list. That way, a love track can play whenever your partner calls, and you know it's them before even looking. Do that by heading to *Phone -> Connections -> tapping the individual whose ringtone you want to improve -> Edit -> Ringtone.*

- *Get Full-Screen Photos for Incoming Phone calls*: The incoming call screen does not have to be boring. With this suggestion, you can view a fullscreen picture of the individual calling you. Go to *Mobile phone -> Connections -> touch the individual -> Edit -> Add Picture.*

- *Customize Text Tone*: Like everyone else can customize the ringtones that play for calls, you can customize the appearance like video when you get texts. Go to *Configurations -> Seems (Noises & Haptics on some models) -> Text message Tone.*

TIPS: You're not limited by the band and text tone that include the iPhone. You can purchase ringtones from Apple, and some applications help you create your tone.

Other iPhone Customization Options

Here's an assortment of a few of our other favorite ways to customize our iPhones.

- *Delete Pre-Installed Apps*: Got a couple of applications pre-installed on your iPhone you don't use? You can delete them (well, the majority of them, anyhow)! Just use the typical way to delete apps: Touch and keep until they tremble, then tap the x on the application icon.

- *Customize Control Center*: Control Center has a lot more options than are apparent initially. Customize Control Center to get just the group of tools you want to use. Head to *Settings -> Control Center -> Customize Settings.*

- *Install your preferred Keyboard*: The iPhone includes an excellent onscreen keypad; nevertheless, you can install third-party keyboards that add cool features, like *Google search, emojis, and GIFs, plus much more.* Get yourself a new keyboard at the App Store, then go to *Settings -> General -> Keyboard -> Keyboards.*

- *Make Siri a friend*: Choose to have Siri talk with you utilizing a man's tone of voice? It could happen. Head to *Settings -> Siri & Search -> Siri Tone of voice -> Male.* You can even go with different accents if you want.

- *Change Browser's default search engine*: Have search engines apart from Google that you'd like to use? Make it the default for those queries in Browser. Head to *Settings -> Browser -> Search Engine and making a fresh selection.*

- *Make Your Shortcuts*: If you an iPhone 8 or newer version user, you can create all sorts of cool customized gestures and shortcuts for various jobs.

- *Jailbreak Your Phone*: To obtain the most control over customizing your mobile phone, you can jailbreak it; this gets rid of Apple's settings over certain types of customization. Jailbreaking can cause functional problems and lessen your phone's security, but it can give more control.

Customize iPhone Home Screen

You may take a look at your iPhone home screen more than some other single screen so that it should be set up the way you want it to appear. Below are a few options for customizing your iPhone home screen.

- *Change Your Wallpaper*: You may make the image behind your applications on the home screen just about whatever you want. A favorite picture of your children or spouse or the logo design of your preferred team is a few options. Find the wallpaper settings by heading to *Settings -> Wallpaper -> Select a New Wallpaper*.

- *Use Live or Video Wallpaper*: Want something eye-catching? Use cartoon wallpapers instead. There are a few restrictions, but this is fairly cool. *Head to Settings -> Wallpaper -> Select a New*

Wallpaper -> pick and choose Active or Live.

- **Put Apps into Folders**: Organize your home screen centred on how you utilize applications by grouping them into folders. Begin by gently tapping and securing one application until all your apps begin to tremble. Then pull and drop one application onto another to place those two applications into a folder.

- **Add Extra Webpages of Apps**: All your apps won't need to be about the same home screen. You may make individual "webpages" for different kinds of applications or different users by tapping and keeping applications or folders, then dragging them from the right side of the screen. Browse the *"Creating Web pages on iPhone"* portion of How to Manage Apps on the iPhone Home Screen to get more.

iPhone Customizations that make things Better to see

It isn't always a simple text message or onscreen items on your iPhone, but these customizations make things much simpler to see.

- _Use Screen Focus_: Do all the onscreen symbols and text message look a little too small for your eye? Screen Move magnifies your iPhone screen automatically. To utilize this option, go to _Settings -> Screen & Brightness -> View -> Zoomed -> Collection._

- _Change Font Size_: The default font size on your iPhone may be a little small for your eye; nevertheless, you can raise it to make reading convenient. Head to *Settings -> General -> Availability -> Larger Text message -> move the slider to On/green -> change the slider below.*

- **Use Dark mode**: If the shiny colors of the iPhone screen strain your eye, you may choose to use Dark Setting, which inverts shiny colors to darker ones. Find the essential Dark settings in *Configurations -> General -> Convenience -> Screen Accommodations -> Invert Colors.*

Customize iPhone Lock Screen

Like everyone else, you can customize your home screen; you can customize the iPhone lock screen, too. In this manner, you have control over the very first thing you see each time you wake up your phone.

- **Customize Lock Screen Wallpaper**: Exactly like

on the home screen, you can transform your iPhone lock screen wallpaper to employ a picture, computer animation, or video. Browse the link within the last section for details.

- **Create a Stronger Passcode**: The much longer your passcode, the harder it is to break right into your iPhone (you are utilizing a passcode, right?). The default passcode is 4 or 6 character types (depending on your iOS version); nevertheless, you make it much longer and stronger. *Head to Settings -> Face ID (or Touch ID) & Passcode -> Change Passcode and following an instructions.*

- **Get Suggestions from Siri**: Siri can learn your practices, preferences, passions, and location and then use that information to suggest content for you. Control what Siri suggests by heading to

Configurations -> Siri & Search -> Siri Recommendations and setting the things you want to use to On/green.

Customize iPhone Notifications

Your iPhone helpfully notifies you to understand when you have calls, text messages, emails, and other bits of information that may interest you. But those notifications can be irritating. Customize how you get notifications with these pointers.

- ***Choose Your Notification Style****: The iPhone enables you to choose lots of notification styles, from simple pop-ups to a mixture of sound and text messages, and more. Find the notification options in *Settings -> Notifications -> touch the application you want to regulate -> choose Alerts, Banner Style, Noises, and more.*

- *Group Notifications from the Same App*: Get yourself many notifications from an individual app, but won't need to see each one taking space on your screen? You can group notifications into a *"stack"* that occupies the same space as your notification. Control this on the per-app basis by heading to *Settings -> Notifications -> the application you want to regulate -> Notification Grouping.*

- *Adobe flashes a Light for Notifications*: Unless you want to try out to get a notification, you may make the camera adobe flashlight instead. It's a delicate, but apparent, option for most situations. Set this up in *Settings -> General -> Convenience -> Hearing -> move the LED Screen for Notifications slider to On/green.*

- *Get Notification Previews with Face ID*: In case your iPhone has Face ID, you can utilize it to keep the notifications private. This establishing shows a simple headline in notifications; however, when you go through the screen and get identified by Face ID, the notification expands, showing more content. Establish this by going to *Settings -> Notifications -> Show Previews -> When Unlocked.*

TIPS: That link also offers an excellent tip about using Face ID to silent alarms, and notification sounds, i.e., *"Reduce Alarm Volume and Keep Screen Shiny with Attention Awareness."*

- *Get more information with Notification Center Widgets*: Notification Center not only gathers all your notifications, but it also offers up widgets,

mini-versions of applications to enable you to do
things without starting apps whatsoever.

Chapter 9

iPhone 8 Gestures You Should Know

Just like the iPhone 7 launched in 2017, the iPhone 8 doesn't include a physical home button, instead deciding on gestures to regulate the new user interface. It would require a couple of days to get used to the change but stay with it. By day three, you'll question how you ever coped without it, and using an "old" iPhone would appear old and antiquated.

1. **Unlock your iPhone 8**: Go through the phone and swipe up from underneath the screen. It truly is that easy, and also you don't need to hold back for the padlock icon at the very top to improve to the unlock visual before swiping up.

2. **Touch to wake**: Tap on your iPhone 8 screen

when it's off to wake it up and find out what notifications you have. To unlock it with FaceID, you'll still have to set it up.

3. **Back to the Homescreen**: Whatever application you are in, if you would like to return to the Home screen, swipe up from underneath of the screen. If you're within an application that is operating scenery, you'll need to keep in mind slipping up from underneath the screen (i.e., the medial side) rather than where, in fact, the Home button used to be.

4. **Have a screenshot**: Press the power button and the volume up button together quickly, and it would snap a screenshot of whatever is on the screen.

5. **Addressing Control Centre:** It used to be always a swipe up, now it's a swipe down from the very best right of the screen. Even if your iPhone doesn't have 3D Touch, you can still long-press on the symbols to gain usage of further configurations within each icon.

6. **Accessing open up apps:** Previously you raise tapped on the home button to uncover what apps you'd open. You now swipe up and then pause with your finger on the screen. After that, you can see the applications you have opened up in the order you opened them.

7. **Launch Siri:** When you may use the "Hey Siri" hot term to awaken Apple's digital associate, there are still ways to release the function utilizing a button press. Press and contain the wake/rest

button on the right aspect of the phone before Siri interface pops-up on screen.

8. **Switch your phone off**: Because long-pressing the wake/rest button launches Siri now, there's a fresh way for switching the phone off. To take action, you would need to press and contain the wake/rest button and the volume down button at the same time. Now glide to power off.

9. **Release Apple Pay**: Again, the wake/rest button is the main element here. Double touch it, and it would talk about your Apple Budget, then scan that person, and it'll request you to keep your phone near to the payment machine.

10. **Gain access to widgets on the lock screen**: Swipe from still left to directly on your lock screen, ideal

for checking your activity bands.

Using Memoji

- **Create your Memoji:** Open up Messages and begin a new meaning. Touch the tiny monkey icon above the keypad, and then strike the "+" button to generate your personality. You would customize face form, skin tone, curly hair colour, eye, jewelry, plus much more.

- **Use your Memoji/Animoji in a FaceTime call:** Take up a FaceTime call, then press the tiny star icon underneath the corner. Now, tap the Memoji you want to use.

- **Memoji your selfies:** So, if you select your Memoji face, preferably to your real to life face, you can send selfies with the Memoji changing your head in Messages. Take up a new message and touch the camera icon, and then press that top button. Now choose the Animoji option by tapping that monkey's mind again. Choose your Memoji and tap the 'x,' not the "done" button, and then take your picture.

- **<u>Record a Memoji video</u>:** Sadly, Memoji isn't available as a choice in the camera app, but that doesn't mean you can't record one. Much like the picture selfie, go to communications, touch on the camera icon and then slip to video and then tap on the superstar. Weight the Animoji or your Memoji, and off you decide to go.

iOS 13 iPhone 8 Notification Tips

- *Notifications collection to provide quietly*: If you're worried that you would be getting way too many notifications, you can place the way they deliver with an app by application basis. Swipe left when you've got a notification on the Lock screen and touch on Manage. Touch Deliver Quietly. Calm notifications come in Notification Centre, but do not show up on the Lock screen, play audio, present a banner or badge the application icon. You've just surely got to be sure you check every once in a while.

- *Switch off notifications from an app*: Same method as the "Deliver Quietly" feature, other than you tap the "Switch off..." option.

- *Open up Notification Centre on Lock screen*: From your lock screen, swipe up from the center of the screen, and you would visit a long set of earlier notifications if you have any.

- *Check Notifications anytime*: To check on your Notifications anytime, swipe down from the very best left part of the screen to reveal them.

Using Screen Time

- *Checking your Screen Time*: You can examine how you've been making use of your phone with the new Screen Time feature in iOS 13. You'll find the reviews in *Configurations > Screen Time.*

- *Scheduled Downtime:* If you want just a little help making use of your mobile phone less, you can restrict what applications you utilize when. Check out Settings > Screen Time and choose the Downtime option. Toggle the change to the "on" position and choose to routine a period when only specific applications and calls are allowed. It's ideal for preventing you or your children from using their cell phones after an arranged time, for example.

- *Set application limits*: App Limitations enable you to choose which group of applications you want to include a period limit to. Choose the category and then "add" before choosing a period limit and striking "plans."

- *Choose "always allowed" apps*: However, you might be willing to lock down your phone to avoid you utilizing it, that's no good if most of your way of getting in touch with people is via an application that gets locked away. Utilize this feature always to allow certain applications whatever limitations you apply.

- *Content & Personal privacy limitations*: This section is also within the primary Screen Time configurations menu and particularly useful if you are a mother or father with kids who use iOS devices. Utilizing it, you can restrict all types of content and options, including iTunes and in-app buys, location services, advertising, etc. It's worth looking at.

Siri shortcuts

- *Siri Shortcuts*: There are several little "help" the iPhone 8 offers via Siri Shortcuts. To start to see the ones recommended for you, go to *Configurations* > *Siri & Search* and choose what you think would be helpful from the automatically produced suggestions. Touch "all shortcuts" to see more. If you wish to install specific "shortcuts" for a variety of different applications that aren't recommended by the iPhone, you can do this by downloading the dedicated Siri Shortcuts.

iPhone 8 Control Centre Tips

- *Add new handles*: Just like the previous version of iOS, you can include and remove handles from Control Centre. Check out *Configurations* > *Control Centre* > *Customise Handles* and then choose which settings you would like to add.

- **_Reorganize handles_**: To improve the order of these settings, you've added, touch, and contain the three-bar menu on the right of whichever control you would like to move, then move it along the list to wherever you would like it to be.

- **_Expand handles_**: Some settings may become full screen, press harder on the control you want to expand, and it will fill the screen.

- **_Activate screen recording_**: Among the new options, you can include regulating Centre is Screen Recording. Be sure you add the control, then open up Control Centre and press the icon that appears like an excellent white circle in the thin white band. To any extent further, it'll record everything that occurs on your screen. Press the control again if you are done, and it will save a video to your Photos application automatically.

- *Adjust light/screen brightness*: You can activate your camera adobe flash, utilizing it as a torch by starting Control Centre and tapping on the torch icon. If you wish to adjust the lighting, power press the icon, then adapt the full-screen slider that shows up.

- *Quickly switch where a sound is played*: One cool feature is the capability to change where music is playing. While music is playing, through Apple Music, Spotify, or wherever, press on the music control or touch the tiny icon in the very best part of the music control; this introduces a pop-up screening available devices that you can play through; this may be linked earphones, a Bluetooth loudspeaker, Apple Television, your iPhone, or any AirPlay device.

- *Set an instant timer*: Rather than going to the timer app, you can force press on the timer icon, then glide up or down on the full-screen to create a timer from about a minute to two hours long.

- *How to gain access to HomeKit devices*: Open up Control Center and then tap on the tiny icon that appears like a home.

iPhone 8 Photos and Camera Tips

- *Enable/disable Smart HDR*: Among the new iPhone's camera advancements is HDR, which helps boost colors, light, and detail in hard light conditions. It's on by default, but if you would like to get it turned on or off, you manually can check out *Settings > Camera and discover the Smart HDR toggle change.*

- **Keep a standard photograph with HDR**: Right under the Smart HDR toggle is a "Keep Normal Photo" option, which would save a regular, no HDR version of your picture as well as the Smart HDR photo.

- **Portrait Lights**: To take Portrait Setting shots with artificial lights, first go to capture in Family portrait mode. Portrait Setting only works for people on the iPhone 8 when capturing with the rear-facing camera. To choose your Portrait Setting capturing style, press and hang on the screen where it says "DAYLIGHT" and then move your finger to the right.

- *Edit Portrait Lights after taking pictures*: Open up any Family portrait shot in Photos and then tap "edit." After another or two, you will see the light effect icon at the bottom of the image, touch it, and swipe just as you did when shooting the image.

- *Edit Portrait setting Depth*: Using the new iPhone 8, you can modify the blur impact after shooting the Portrait shot. Check out Photos and choose the picture you want to regulate, then select "edit." You will see a depth slider at the bottom of the screen. Swipe to boost the blur strength, swipe left to diminish it.

- *How exactly to Merge People in Photos app*: Photos in iOS can check out your photos and identify people and places. If you discover that the application has chosen the same person, but says they vary, you can combine the albums collectively. To get this done, go directly to the Photos application > Albums and choose People & Places. Touch on the term "Select" at the very top right of the screen and then choose the images of individuals you want to merge, then tap "merge."

- **Remove people in Photos app**: Head to Photos App, Albums, and choose People & Places. To eliminate tap on "Choose" and then tap on individuals you do not want to see before tapping on "Remove" underneath still left of your iPhone screen.

iPhone 8: Keyboard Tips

- **Go one-handed**: iOS 13's QuickType keypad

enables you to type one-handed, which is fantastic on the larger devices like the iPhone 8 and XS Greatest extent. Press and contain the emoji or world icon and then keypad configurations. Select either the still left or right-sided keypad. It shrinks the keypad and techniques it to 1 aspect of the screen. Get back to full size by tapping the tiny arrow.

- *Use your keyboard as a trackpad*: Previously, with 3D Touch shows, you utilize the keyboard area as a trackpad to go the cursor on the screen. You'll still can, but it works just a little in a different way here, rather than pressure pressing anywhere on the keypad, press, and hangs on the spacebar instead.

Face ID Tips

- *Adding another in-person ID*: if you regularly change appearance now, you can put in a second In person ID to state the iPhone 8 getting puzzled. That is also really useful if you would like to add your lover to allow them to use your mobile phone while you're traveling, for example.

iPhone 8: Screen Tips

- *Standard or Zoomed screen*: Since iPhone 6 Plus, you've had the opportunity to select from two quality options. You can transform the screen settings from Standard or Zoomed on the iPhone 8 too. To change between your two - if you have changed your mind after set up - go to

Configurations > Screen & Lighting > Screen Focus and choose Standard or Zoomed.

- ***Enable True Tone screen***: If you didn't get it done at the step, you could transform it anytime. To get the iPhone's screen to automatically change its color balance and heat to complement the background light in the area, check out Control Centre and push press the screen lighting slider. Now touch the True Firmness button. You can even go to *Configurations > Screen and Lighting* and toggle the *"True Shade"* switch.

iPhone 8 Battery Tips

- *Check your average battery consumption*: In iOS 13, you can check out Settings > Battery, and you will see two graphs. One shows the electric battery level; the other shows your screen on and screen off activity. You would find two tabs. One shows your last day; the other turns up to fourteen days; this way, you can view how energetic your phone battery strength and breakdowns screening your average screen on and off times show under the graphs.

- *Enable Low-Power Mode*: The reduced Power Mode (Settings > Electric battery) enables you to reduce power consumption. The feature disables or reduces history application refresh, auto-downloads, email fetch, and more (when allowed). You can turn it on at any point, or you are prompted to carefully turn it on at the 20 and 10 % notification markers. You can even put in control to regulate Centre and get access to it quickly by swiping up to gain access to Control Center and tapping on the electric battery icon.

- *Find electric battery guzzling apps*: iOS specifically lets you know which apps are employing the most power. Head to Configurations > Electric battery and then scroll right down to the section that provides you an in-depth look at all of your battery-guzzling apps.

- *Check your battery via the Electric battery widget*: Inside the widgets in Today's view, some cards enable you to start to see the battery life staying in your iPhone, Apple Watch, and linked headphones. Just swipe from left to directly on your Home screen to access your Today view and scroll until you start to see the "Batteries" widget.

- *Charge wirelessly*: To utilize the iPhone's wifi charging capabilities, buy a radio charger. Any Qi charger will continue to work, but to charge more effectively, you will need one optimized for Apple's 7.5W charging.

- *Fast charge it*: When you have a 29W, 61W, or 87W USB Type-C power adapter for a MacBook, you can plug in your iPhone 8 Pro utilizing a Type-C to Lightning wire watching it charge quickly. Up to 50 % in thirty minutes.

Chapter 10

Useful iPhone 8 Tips & Tricks

Control Your Apple TV With iPhone 8

The Control Focus on the iPhone 8 has an awesome trick: it enables you to regulate your Apple TV if you have one. So long as your iPhone 8 and Apple Television are on a single cellular network, it'll work. Get into Control Center and then look for the Apple Television button that shows up. Touch it and start managing your Apple Television.

How to Enable USB Limited Setting on iPhone 8

Apple just built a robust new security feature into the iPhone 8 with the latest version of iOS; this launch is what's known as **USB Limited Setting** to the iPhone 8.

Lately, companies have been making devices that may be connected to an iPhone's USB slot and crack an iPhone's passcode.

To protect from this, Apple has introduced a USB Restricted Setting. USB Restricted Setting disabled data writing between an iPhone and a USB device if the iPhone is not unlocked to get more than one hour; this effectively makes the iPhone breaking boxes ineffective as they may take hours or times to unlock a locked iPhone.

By default, *USB Limited Mode* is enabled in iOS. But for those who want to disable it, or make sure it hasn't been disabled, go to the *Configurations app* and touch *Face ID & Passcode*. Enter your passcode and then swipe down until you visit a section entitled *"Allow Access When Locked."*

The final toggle in this section is a field that says *"USB Accessories."* The toggle next to them should be turned OFF (white); this implies *USB Restricted Setting* is allowed, and devices can't download or upload data from/to your iPhone if the iPhone is not unlocked to get more than one hour.

Use Two Pane Scenery View

This tip only pertains to the iPhone 8 Pro Max but is cool nonetheless. If you keep your XS device horizontally when using specific applications, you'll see lots of the built-in apps changes to a two-pane setting, including Email and Records. This setting is the main one you observe on an iPad where, for example, you can see a list of all of your records in the Records app while positively reading or editing a single note.

How to stop iPhone 8 Alarms with Your Face

An extremely cool feature of the iPhone 8 is Face ID. It gives you to unlock your phone just by taking a look at it. Face ID also has various other cool features-like that one. Whenever your iPhone 8 or XS security alarm goes off, you could silent it by just picking right up your iPhone and taking a look at it; this tells your iPhone you understand about the arm, and it'll quiet it.

Quickly Disable Face ID

Depending on your geographical area, the police might be able to legally demand you uncover your smartphone at that moment via its facial recognition features. For reasons unknown, facial biometrics aren't protected in the manner fingerprints, and passcodes are; in a few localities. That's why Apple has generated an attribute that lets you quickly disable Face ID in a pinch without going into your settings. Just press the side button five times, and Face ID will be disabled, and you'll need to enter your passcode instead to gain access to your phone.

How decelerate the two times click necessary for Apple Pay

Given that the iPhone 8 jettisoned the Touch ID sensor, you confirm your *Apple Pay* obligations by using Face ID and twice pressing the medial side button. By default, you would need to dual press the medial side button pretty quickly-but it is possible to make things slow down.

To take action, go to *Settings > General > Availability.* Now scroll right down to Side Button. Privately Button screen, you can select between *default, gradual, or slowest.* Pick the speed that is most effective for you.

Chapter 11

How to Fix Common iPhone 8 Problems

iPhone 8 Touch Screen Issues

The bright, beautiful *"edge-to-edge"* OLED screen on the iPhone is one of its major new features; however, the touch screen may sometimes go wrong. Both most common situations are:

✓ *Non-responsive* *SCREEN* *AND* *"GHOST TOUCHES."*

Some users state that the screen on the iPhone 8 sometimes halts working. In those instances, the screen doesn't react to details or touches. In other situations, the contrary occurs: "ghost details" appear to activate things on the screen even when they don't touch it.

If you are experiencing either of these issues, the reason

is the same: a hardware problem with the touch screen chips and detectors in the iPhone 8; because these problems are the effect of a hardware issue, you can't fix them yourself. Fortunately, Apple knows the problem and offers to repair it. Find out about how to proceed on Apple's web page about the problem.

✓ *FROZEN Screen IN WINTER*

A different type of iPhone 8 screen problem that many people run into would be that the screen freezes up and becomes unresponsive for a couple of seconds when going from a warm spot to a chilly one (such as moving out into a wintery day). The good thing is that this is not a hardware problem, so it is much simpler to fix. Try out these quick DIY fix:

- *Update the iOS*: This issue was set with the iOS

11.1.2 update, so make sure you're operating that version of the operating system or higher.

- *Follow Apple's Cold-Weather Recommendations*: Apple has tips and recommendations for the temperatures to use the iPhone in, it suggests not using it in temperature ranges less than 32 degrees F (0 degrees C). Having your iPhone within your clothes and near to your body, warmth is an excellent, simple fix.

iPhone 8 Loudspeaker Problems

The iPhone is a great multimedia device; however, many users report reduced enjoyment of media on the iPhone 8 credited to speaker problems. Listed below are two of the very most common.

a) SPEAKERS Audio MUFFLED

Speakers whose audio is quiet than they ought to, or whose audio sounds muffled, can frequently be fixed by doing the next:

- *Restart iPhone*: Restarting your iPhone can solve all types of problems, including sound issues.

- *Clean the Speakers*. You might have dirt or other gunk developed on the loudspeakers that are leading to the quietness. Understand how to completely clean iPhone speakers.

- *Check the Case*: If you are using a case with your iPhone, make sure there is nothing stuck between your case and the loudspeaker, like pocket lint, that may be causing the problem.

b) Loudspeaker CRACKLES at high volume

Around the other end of the range, some iPhone 8 users have reported that their speakers make a distressing crackling sound when their volume is too high. If this is going on for you, try the next steps:

- *Restart iPhone*: It might not assist in this case, but it's fast and straightforward so that it never hurts to get one of this restart. You can also get one of these hard reset if you want.

- *Update the OS*: Because the latest version of the iOS also includes the latest bug fixes, make sure you're operating it.

- *Talk with Apple*: Crackling loudspeakers are likely to be always a hardware problem that you can't solve. Get active support from Apple instead.

Some individuals have encountered problems

using Wi-Fi on the iPhone 8. This probably isn't a concern with the iPhone 8 itself. Much more likely, this has regarding software configurations or your Wi-Fi network. Find out about the complexities and fixes in How exactly to Fix an iPhone That Can't Hook up to Wi-Fi in other recommended books at the end of this book.

iPhone 8 Charging Problems

The iPhone 8 is the first iPhone to add support for wireless charging. That's cool, but it isn't cool if the telephone won't charge properly. If you are facing that problem, try these steps to repair it:

- *Get one of these New Charging Wire*: Maybe the charging problem has been your wire, not your phone. Try another wire you know for certain works. Make especially certain to either use the official Apple wire or one that's qualified by Apple.

- **_Remove Credit cards From Case_**: If you are wanting to charge cellular and have an instance that also stores things such as credit cards, take away the credit cards. The cellular payment top features of the credit cards can hinder the cellular charging.

- **_Remove Case for Wifi Charging_**: Removing the whole case may be considered a good idea if you are charging wirelessly. Not absolutely all cases are appropriate for cellular charging, so that they may be avoiding normal function.

- **_Restart iPhone_**: You never know very well what types of problems a restart can solve. This may be one of them.

iPhone 8 Electric battery Life Problems

There is nothing worse than not having the ability to use your mobile phone because it's working out of electric battery too early, but that's the thing some users complain about. And with most of its fresh, power-hungry features - the OLED screen, for example - it isn't a shock that there could be some iPhone 8 electric battery problems.

Fortunately, battery issues on the iPhone are simple enough to solve using the settings included in iOS. Below are a few tips:

- *Learn to Preserve Battery*: There are over 30+ tips about how to raise your iPhone's electric battery life. Use a few of these as well as your iPhone would run much longer between charges.

- *Update the OS*: Furthermore, to fix a bug, new variations of iOS often deliver improvements that make the battery better. Install the latest revise, and you'll see your electric battery last longer.

- *Get a protracted Life Electric battery*: Maybe the simplest way to get your electric battery to go longer is to obtain additional battery. There are sorts of prolonged life batteries on the marketplace, from exterior dongles to others.

iPhone 8 Face ID Problems

Most likely, the single coolest feature of the iPhone 8 is the facial ID, the facial recognition system. This feature is utilized for security and convenience: it unlocks the telephone, can be used to enter passwords, and even authorizes Apple Pay transactions. But issues with Face ID and either front or back camera can cause your iPhone

8 never to identify you. If you are (ahem) facing this issue, try these pointers:

- *Adjust iPhone Position*: If Face ID sometimes identifies you, but other times doesn't, consider changing the position you're holding the telephone. As the Face ID sensors are relatively sophisticated, they need to be capable of getting a good view of that person to work.

- *Clean "The Notch."*: THE FACIAL ID detectors are situated in "the notch," the deep cut-out near the top of the screen. If those receptors get protected with dirt or even enough oil from your skin layer, their standard procedure could be reduced. Try wiping "the notch" clean.

- *Update the OS*: Apple regularly enhances the

speed and precision of Face ID, as well as fixes insects, in new variations of the iOS. If you are having Face ID problems on iPhone 8, make sure you're using the latest operating system.

- *Reset Face ID*: The problem is probably not with Face ID itself, but instead with the initial scans of that person created when you set up Face ID to start. If the other activities haven't helped, be rid of your old face scans and make new ones. Enter a shiny, well-lit place and then go to Configurations -> Face ID & Passcode -> enter your passcode -> Reset Face ID. Then create Face ID from scratch.

- *Contact Apple*: If none of the things has helped, there may be a problem with the hardware in your iPhone 8 (maybe it's a problem with the video cameras, the Face ID sensors, or another thing). If so, you should contact Apple to obtain an analysis of the problem and a fix.

- *You might have seen tales on the internet claiming that Face ID has been hacked*: They are virtually all bogus. Face ID can be an extremely advanced system that depends on thousands of data factors to identify a face. Yes, similar twins might be able to beat Face ID (it seems sensible; they have simply the same face!). Other families that look nearly the same as one another can also be able to technique it. But also, for the most part, the probability of Face ID being tricked or hacked is very, surprisingly low.

iPhone 8 Screen Issues

The iPhone 8 was the first iPhone to use the brighter, better OLED screen technology. The screen appears excellent, but it's susceptible to some issues that other iPhones using different systems aren't. Perhaps most obviously among these is "burn off in."; this happens when the same image is shown on a screen for an extended period, resulting in faint "spirits" of these images showing up on the screen regularly, regardless of what else has been screened. Fortunately, OLED burn-in is simple to avoid. Just follow these pointers:

- *Lower Screen Lighting*: The low the lighting of your screen, the less likely a graphic burn off involved with it. You have two options here. First, you can by hand reduce your screen brightness by starting Control Center and moving the lighting slider down. On the other hand, let your screen brightness change to ambient light by heading to *Configurations -> General -> Convenience -> Screen brightness -> Auto-Brightness.*

- *Set Screen to Auto-Lock*: Burn off happens when a graphic is on the screen for an extended period. So, if your screen hair and shuts off regularly, the image can't burn off. Set your screen to lock by heading to Configurations automatically -> Screen & Lighting -> Auto-Lock and choose five minutes or less.

Another screen problem that impacts some iPhone 8 models is a green line that appears at the right edge of the screen. That is another hardware problem that users can't fix themselves. If you see this, your very best wager is to get hold of Apple to get active support.

CHAPTER 12

How to Use iPhone 8 Series Portrait Settings to Make Blurry Background

The **iPhone 8 Series (iPhone 8 plus) portrait mode** is the correct device to make brilliant looking portrait photographs with your iPhone 8 Series (iPhone 8 plus). The portrait setting gives you to quickly produce a shallow depth of field in your pictures. This leads to an excellent blurry background that could typically be performed with a **DSLR camera**. With this section, you'll see how to use the iPhone 8 Series (iPhone 8 plus) portrait setting to make a professional-looking iPhone 8 Series (iPhone 8 plus) photo with a beautiful background blur.

What's Portrait Mode?

Portrait mode is a distinctive capturing mode available in the native camera application of an iPhone 8 Series (iPhone 8 plus). It creates use of a unique **Depth Impact Tool** to make a shallow Depth of field in your pictures.

Shallow depth of field means that only a little area of the photo is within focus as the other is blurred. More often than not, you'll need your most significant concern at the mercy of appearing in razor-sharp focus as the background shows up blurred.

This soft and tender blurry background is categorized as "bokeh," which originates from the Japanese language.

Why should we use a Shallow Depth of Field?

The **shallow depth of Field** is often utilized by portrait photographers. Why? Since it places the focus on the average person and creates a sensitive, dreamy backdrop in it. Blurring the context is also truly useful when taking in locations with a busy, messy, or distracting backdrop. The blurring makes the context secondary, getting the viewer's attention back to the principal subject matter in the foreground.

Shallow Depth of Field isn't something you'd use for every kind of picture. You typically wouldn't want a blurry Background in scenery or architectural picture as you'd want to see everything vividly from foreground to Background.

However, in portrait pictures, a Shallow Depth of Field can make a significant distinction to the result of your photo. By blurring the backdrop, you may make your subject matter stand out.

How to Develop Background Blur Using an iPhone 8 Series (iPhone 8 plus)

Sometimes back, the iPhone 8 Series (iPhone 8 plus) camera hasn't allowed you to have any control over the depth of field for your pictures. You've had the choice to have everything in Focus - unless your most significant subject matter comes very near the zoom lens, in such case the backdrop seems blurred.

However, with portrait setting on the new iPhone 8 Series (iPhone 8 plus), now you can pick and choose what's in focus and what isn't. This gives you unprecedented control over your iPhone 8 Series (iPhone

8 plus) camera, permitting you to mimic the appearance of DSLR cameras that can catch a shallow depth of field.

While portrait mode is most beneficial when planning on taking pictures of humans, pets, nature, etc., it can be utilized to blur the backdrop behind any subject.

Many things appear better when there's a soft, dreamy background in it - especially if that background could distract the viewer from the primary subject.

How to use iPhone Portrait Mode

- Developing a shallow **Depth of Field** with Portrait mode on the iPhone is super easy. You can start by starting the default camera app, then swipe through the taking pictures modes (video, picture, etc.) until Portrait is highlighted in yellow.

- The very first thing you'll notice when you switch

to Portrait Setting is that everything gets enlarged. That's because the camera automatically switches to the iPhone's 2x Telephoto Zoom lens. The telephoto zoom lens typically creates more flattering portrait images than the huge-angle zoom lens that could distort cosmetic features.

- You'll additionally spot the words **Depth Impact** appears in the bottom of the screen. Moreover, your telephone will help you giving on-screen instructions in case you don't have things framed up optimally for an enjoyable portrait shot. For instance, you'll possibly see Move Farther Away or even more Light Required:

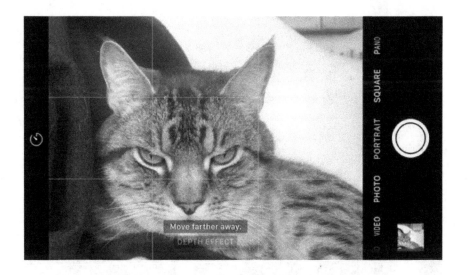

- The moment you're at the right distance from your subject, the words **Depth Effect** would be highlighted in yellow. You'll also see four yellow crop marks, indicating the face of your subject:

- You're now ready to take, so select the shutter button to consider your picture. After making the picture, you'll observe that two variations of the image can look in the camera app. One image will have the *Depth Impact* (blurred Background) and the other won't.

- Evaluating those two versions of the image sincerely suggests how nice a portrait picture shows up when it has a **Shallow Depth of Field**.

- If for reasons unknown you're not sure which of both pictures had the **Depth impact**, it'll be labelled in your image Set as shown below:

Tips For Creating Awesome Background Blur

When taking pictures with the iPhone portrait mode, it's

essential to think about your background plus your subject. The type of Background you choose against its distance from your subject matter, will each have a significant effect on the final image.

The **Depth Effect** in Portrait mode is most effective when your subject matter is not the backdrop. The further away the topic is from the backdrop, the more delightful blur you'll get. Spot the difference in the backdrop blur of the two pictures:

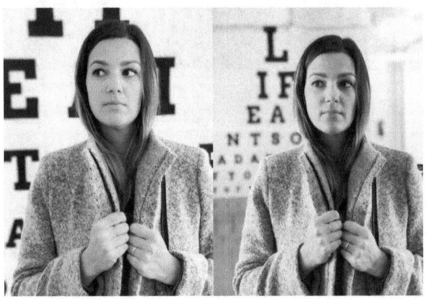

Subject close to background   Subject farther away from background

So; if your Background doesn't show up blurry enough when taking photos in a portrait setting, move your subject matter further from the background.

It's additionally essential to have something in the backdrop so that there are a few components for the camera to blur.

Conclusively; the iPhone 8 Series (iPhone 8 plus) has continuously been a first-rate device for most types of picture taking - such as landscape, structures, and street picture taking. However, now the iPhone 8 Series (iPhone 8 plus) provides potential to take amazing, high-quality portrait photos.

The telephoto zoom lens on the iPhone 8 Series (iPhone 8 plus) is more flattering for shooting people than the typical wide-angle zoom lens.

As well as the **Magical Depth Impact tool** in the iPhone

8 Series (iPhone 8 plus) Portrait Mode creates lovely background blur - simulating the shallow depth of field that could formerly only be performed with a DSLR camera.

Taking photos with the iPhone 8 Series (iPhone 8 plus) portrait mode is a delight. Moreover, your subject will be thrilled when you suggest to them how beautiful they show up on your photos.

Don't forget; even while Portrait mode is the perfect setting when planning on taking pictures of individuals, pets, nature, etc., you can use it on any subject matter in which you require to make an attractive **background blur**.

CHAPTER 13

Secret iPhone Camera Features Strange to You

Do you want to make the full use of your iPhone 8 Series (iPhone 8 plus) camera when you take photographs? As it's easy to take a photo with your iPhone, the excellent and crucial iPhone digital camera features are hidden from regular iPhone users. So, in this section, you'll find out the concealed iPhone camera features that every iPhone users must use.

- Swipe Left for Swift Access to Your iPhone Camera. How often have you seen or witness an incredible scene in front of your eyes, only to discover that it's gone at the time you're prepared to take a photo? You can improve your possibilities of taking a perfect shot if you know how to use your camera effectively.

- In case your iPhone is locked, you can press the home button to wake up your phone, and then swipe left through the lock display.

- The camera would open immediately, and you won't even need to enter your password to unlock your iPhone 8 Series (iPhone 8 plus). This trick would make you begin capturing in less than a second!

- However, what if you're already making use of the iPhone, and also you want to quickly access the digital camera, swipe up from the lower part of the screen to open the Control Center as shown below.

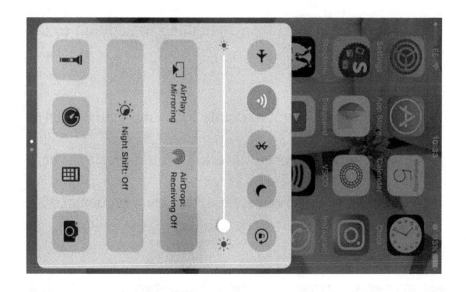

From here, select the camera icon in the bottom right, and you're ready to start taking pictures!

How to Set Focus and Exposure

If you haven't set focus and exposure, the iPhone 8 Series (iPhone 8 plus) can do it for you automatically. Usually, it can be a reasonably good job. Furthermore, that's how most iPhone users take almost all their photographs.

There are a few times, though, when autofocus fails - or

when you wish to Focus on something in addition to the apparent subject.

That's when you'll want to create focus manually. That is super easy to do - Tap the location on the display where you'd prefer to set Focus, and the camera deals with others.

What distinction does the *focus* make? If you go through the picture above, the Focus is defined on the blossom in the foreground. The topic is bright and shiny, as the bloom petals and leaves in the backdrop are blurred.

When you Tap on the screen to set Focus, the camera automatically sets the exposure. The exposure refers to improving the brightness of an image. So it's essential to get the exposure right if you are taking your picture.

*NB: When you wish to set **Focus**, check out the display to find out if the lighting of the image appears suitable. If it seems too vibrant or too darkish, you can change exposure before taking the picture.*

After you've Tapped on the screen to create focus and exposure, the exposure slider with a sun icon would be observed. Swipe up to help make the picture brighter or right down to make the image darker.

Efficaciously setting focus and exposure is one of the primary element skills that a photographer must master. When it takes merely a few Taps to modify focus and exposure, it's essential that you do it effectively to Focus on the most crucial components of the complete picture.

The task is that every photograph takes a specific method of focus and exposure setting.

Things that work notably for landscapes don't work almost as properly for night or tour photos.

How to Lock Focus and Exposure with AE/AF Lock

The iPhone also allows you to lock each one of the appealing points; focus and exposure. So why would you need to lock those functions while going for a picture?

- The principle motive is if anything changes in the scene, including a moving subject or altered lighting, your focus and exposure would stay unchanged.

- That's why it's a great idea to lock Focus and exposure when you're expecting motion within the picture. For instance, *Focus and exposure* lock could be beneficial in street picture taking.

- You might frame the shot, and set the focus and exposure earlier, then obviously watch out for a person to pass-by before taking your photo.

- Once you've locked the focus and exposure, you might take several pictures of the same picture and never have to set focus and exposure each time you want to consider photos. To unlock Focus and exposure, select anywhere on the screen.

- To lock focus and exposure, Tap and retain your hands on the display screen for mere multiple seconds at the stage where you want to create the center point. A yellowish package with AE/AF lock can look near the top of the display.

Note: You can nevertheless swipe up or down on display to regulate exposure manually.

Now regardless of what happens within the framework or how you fling the iPhone 8 plus, the **Focus and Exposure** *would still be unchanged.*

How to Take HDR Photos

HDR, which means *High Active Range*, is another incredible picture tool that is included in the camera of your iPhone 8 plus.

HDR picture taking with the iPhone combines three unique exposures of precisely the same image to produce one nicely exposed picture.

It's exquisite for high comparison moments with shiny and darkish areas since it allows you to fully capture extra component in both shadows and the highlights.

Some small adjustments within an editing application such as Snapseed can indeed draw out the colours and detail that were captured in the **HDR photograph**, although it still comes with fantastic well-balanced exposure.

- You'll find the HDR setting at the left side of the camera app. Tapping on HDR provides you with three options: Motion, ON, or OFF.

- Notably, it's high-quality to use HDR for panorama or landscape pictures and scenes where the sky occupies a significant area of the photograph. This enables the taking of extra fine detail in both brighter sky and the darker foreground.

- There are a few downsides to HDR, especially in conditions of pictures of motion. Because HDR is a variety of three sequentially captured photos, you might encounter "ghosts" if the picture is changing quickly. HDR images also require a long period to capture, which means that your hands may shake even while the shutter is open up.

- It's additionally essential to state that non-HDR pictures will sometimes look much better than HDR ones, that's the reason it's a good idea to save lots of each variation of the picture. To make sure that each variant is stored, go to configurations > photos & camera, and ensure Save Normal Picture is **ON** in the *HDR section*.

- It's also well worth mentioning that the default iPhone 8 Series (iPhone 8 plus) camera application comes with an alternatively subtle *HDR impact*. A sophisticated camera application that can create much more powerful HDR results and provide you with complete control over the catch.

How to Take Snapshot in Burst Mode

- Burst mode is one of the very most useful capturing features in the iPhone 8 Series (iPhone 8 plus)'s camera app. It enables you to take ten images in only one second, which makes it easy to fully capture the suitable movement shot with reduced blur.

- If you wish to activate a *burst setting*, press down

the shutter button for half a second or longer, and the iPhone begins capturing one after another. When you've shot a burst of snap photos, after that, you can choose the lovely images from the Set and delete others.

- Burst setting is worth using each time there's any movement or unpredictability in the picture.

Remember utilizing it when photographing kids, animals, birds, and splashing water.

It's also excellent for taking pictures on magical occasions in street picture taking. Likewise, try the utilization of burst setting to capture the correct stride or present.

How to Take Pictures with Volume Buttons

Perhaps you have ever overlooked or missed the iPhone's tiny on-display shutter button? If so, change to the utilization of volume control keys beside your iPhone 8 plus!

Either of these buttons can be utilized for shutter release, and the tactile opinions you get from pressing this button is a great deal more pleasurable than pressing an electronic switch.

Additionally, this enables you to carry the iPhone with two hands, just as you'd grab a typical digital camera.

The only drawback of the approach is that you'll require pressing the Volume button pretty hard, which might produce camera shake. That's especially essential in a low-mild or less lighted environment, where any movement of your iPhone 8 Series (iPhone 8 plus) would lead to the blurry picture.

How to take Photographs with your Apple Headphones

Remember those white apple headphones that were included with your iPhone 8 plus, on purchase can be utilized for photo taking. This additionally has *Volume buttons*, and you may use these control keys to consider photos!

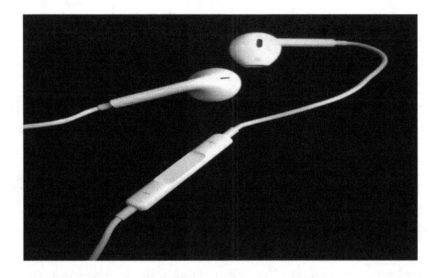

This feature is tremendously useful when you need to take discreet pictures of people you don't recognize or know in person, as you could pretend to be paying focused attention to music or making a call while you're taking pictures.

This method additionally is available when your iPhone 8 Series (iPhone 8 plus) is on a tripod. As you release the shutter with your headphones, you can get rid of any unintentional digital camera movement, which is quite essential for night time pictures, long exposure images, etc.

Chapter 14

5 Ways of Upgrading Your iPhone Digital Photography for Instagram

1. Minimalism is Key

Our number 1 Instagram photography suggestion is to consider photos that look great and professional with your iPhone; you would need to believe. Why? Because it is not only better - but it's much simpler to choose one exciting subject matter and make that the center point of your image.

The sure sign of the amateur is a person who tries to match so many subjects to their imagery. "But my image would be filled with vacant space!" you may protest. That's flawlessly fine. Professional photographers call bare space, *'negative space'*, which is another technique which makes your center point stand out.

The ultimate way to do this is to go closer to the topic and remove anything in the shot that may distract the viewer.

This can make your Instagram photography appear to be like it was done by an expert. As you keep up to apply this, you'll come to find that minimalism is the most shared on systems like Instagram, because photos with ONE center point stick out on smartphone screens.

2. **Get low in Position**

Understandably, your camera move shouldn't be filled with selfies. Just as your camera move shouldn't contain images used at chest elevation.

Among the quickest ways to update your Instagram digital photography and create images that stick out is to take from a lesser position than what you're used to. You don't need to get too low either, capture from less than what you're used to.

When you take your subject or centre point from such a minimal angle that the sky is the only background, what you finish up doing is following both Instagram picture taking Tip 1 and Tip 2 - making the image extremely attractive on the system like Instagram.

So when you're finally more comfortable with the thought of looking, "extra" according to some people, you'll be able to start squatting and even kneeling to be able to get the best low-angle images.

3. Depth of Field

Exactly what does *"depth of field"* mean? Blurring backgrounds, of course! Everyone knows an image with blur looks a lot more interesting than a graphic where the background and the foreground are both in concentration.

When you utilize zoom lens accessories to mention a feeling of depth in your images, i.e. Telephoto lenses, you'll be able to attract people's attention - whether you're photographing accessories for Instagram, or just taking a scenery photograph.

Besides getting hold of iPhone accessories, a straightforward technique like using "leading lines" that direct the audiences' focus on whatever it is that has been photographed is a superb way to produce depth for your Instagram digital photography. For instance, going for a picture of the road, railway track, a riverbank, fences, and pathways are an excellent leading line!

Once you have found your leads, you can create some depth in the foreground by using found items like stones or leaves or other things, for example, When you absolutely cannot find anything in the foreground that could add a component appealing, then get back to Suggestion #2 and "Get Low in position"! Take from a lesser angle, and you will be amazed what you can catch.

4. Get Up-Close and Personal

Okay, so right now, you've probably determined that each of the tips accumulates from the prior tips so that by enough time you've mastered this whole list, you're practically an expert!

Your Instagram picture taking needs details! It might be hard to trust, but a great deal of iPhone professional photographers make the error of not getting close enough to the centre point. Particularly when they're photographing something with a great deal of fine detail - i.e. When you capture from a long distance, the picture eventually ends up being a little dull and impersonal; however, when you get near to the thing, you all of a sudden have an image that involves life - particularly when you take portraits of others or even your selfies. When you move nearer to the subject, you can properly catch cosmetic features and feelings that would build relationships with the viewer.

Even the newer iPhones remain unable to shoot HQ images of subject matter close up and personal, so our reward Instagram photography suggestion is that you would have to get your hands on the macro zoom lens, like the *TrueLux macro zoom lens*.

What this zoom lens can do is allow your camera to target incredibly near to whatever you're shooting and then add visual interest (and depth) to your photograph, simultaneously.

5. Don't Be Scared of the Silhouette

That one seems just like a no-brainer, but many individuals continue to be afraid to embrace silhouettes on the Instagram grid.

First of all, *what is a silhouette? It's mostly when an object's form is captured against a gleaming light. It's not the same thing as a shadow.*

Silhouettes add an air of secret to an image, and against

an extremely bright background, a silhouette really can look quite beautiful on your Instagram feed!

Another best part concerning this particular Instagram photography technique is that it is really simple to create images of a silhouette on your iPhone. You just need to know what you want to take a picture of, and then capture towards the light. That's it!

If you'd like to ensure that your subject's silhouette looks unmistakable but still dark, check out your iPhone camera app, tap the screen to create the focus, and then swipe right down to darken the camera exposure - you can still darken the subject even further with photography editing apps.

The optimum time to consider silhouette photographs, despite having your iPhone, is during what professional photographers refer to as the *golden hours of sunrise and sunset.* When sunlight is low coming, then you can position the source of light behind the topic, which means that you'll get a perfectly coloured sky as the backdrop - taking benefit of tips 1 to 4.

You do not necessarily have to hold back for the golden hour to consider silhouette photographs, so long as your source of light is behind the subject.

For instance, if you are shooting indoors, you merely have to put your subject before the window (to consider advantage of daylight), or before a band light/ softbox if daylight is no option.